The Hat-Stand Union

CAROLINE BIRD is an award-winning poet. She won a major Eric Gregory Award in 2002 and was shortlisted for the Geoffrey Dearmer Prize in 2001. Her first collection, *Looking Through Letter-boxes*, was published in 2002 (when she was just fifteen). She was shortlisted for the Dylan Thomas Prize in 2008 and 2010 for her second and third collections, *Trouble Came to the Turnip* and *Watering Can* (which received a Poetry Book Society Recommendation), on both occasions being the youngest writer on the list. She was one of the five official poets for the London 2012 Olympics; her poem 'The Fun Palace', which celebrates the life and work of Joan Littlewood, is now erected on the Olympic site outside the main stadium.

She is also a playwright. In February 2012 her children's musical *The Trial of Dennis the Menace* was premiered at the Southbank Centre, and in the autumn her radical new version of Euripides' *The Trojan Women* enjoyed a seven-week run at the Gate Theatre, to wide critical acclaim.

Also by Caroline Bird from Carcanet Press

Looking Through Letterboxes
Trouble Came to the Turnip
Watering Can

CAROLINE BIRD

The Hat-Stand Union

CARCANET

Acknowledgements

'The Fun Palace' was commissioned by Winning Words as part of the Art in the Park programme for the London Olympics 2012.

'Public Detectives' was first published in *Joining Music with Reason* (Waywiser Press, 2010), an anthology edited by Christopher Ricks.

Versions of 'Hey Las Vegas' and 'Thoughts inside a Head inside a Kennel inside a Church' were first published online by *Poetry International*, and 'Break-up Party' was published in *Fourteen*.

First published in Great Britain in 2013 by
Carcanet Press Limited
Alliance House
Cross Street
Manchester M2 7AQ

www.carcanet.co.uk

A CIP catalogue record for this book is available from the British Library

ISBN 978 1 84777 164 3

The publisher acknowledges financial assistance from Arts Council England

Supported by
ARTS COUNCIL
ENGLAND

Typeset by XL Publishing Services, Exmouth
Printed and bound in England by SRP Ltd, Exeter

Contents

1 Mystery Tears

2 The Truth about Camelot

3   Sea Bed

For my Mum

1

Mystery Tears

Everything I touch is turning to gold – well, not *real* gold.
– Frank Kuppner

Sealing Wax

Sometimes I think of you,
my funny prodigy
and, like an ashtray on a Bible,

I pose here defeated,
singing 'Lust's most sacred impulse
is error!' to a lean, dark and handsome

hat-stand. I find my head is able
to process a lifetime of gin, carping
'My abuser can be so capricious!' at social workers.

My phone-line is coy as the pale string
unspooling from the back-

end of a goldfish, elsewhere in an empty house.
Sometimes, my stable friend,
I think of you and whether

your bedroom was warm through the winter
and who's spreading vapour rub on your chest.

Some people call me *The Ash Woman*,
or *Gjest Haraldes*, the royal jailbird, and I've been
compared to Peter Christen Baardsen, the philandering
pianist. I have never been to Oslo. I have never set foot
in Nidaros Cathedral in Trondheim. In fact, I've never been
to Norway. But some people call me *Codeine the Wanderer*.

Some people call me *Duchess Mary Adelaide of Speck*
or *Queen Maud of Lancaster Gardens*, I arouse deep rushes
of ceremonialism in women of low rank. In campfire songs
I am named *the cult of Vesta*. I'm not a cult. I'm a small person.
I rarely leave my room. But some crooners call me *Smack the Wife*.

Some people call me *The Red-Handed Virgin*, *Sheeba of Dorwich*,
Jack the Lamp. They say I had a morganatic marriage to a hobo,
he was buried with his trolley and I didn't inherit one tin-can.
In folklore, I've become *Nay Winkatmen* – the very standoffish
prostitute. I am not the saviour of modern thatching
the locals of Wrafton near Brauton in North Devon think I am.

The Jewish Rastafarians call me *Shrunken MC*
for the beatific cakewalk of what used to be – in my youth –
the Crystal Methodist Church, some people call me *Rabbi Marley*.
I am not religious. I have no guiding star. Yet the Vatican engraved
Child of Jilted Joseph on an apostle spoon, jammed it in my sorbet.
My equestrian statue in northwestern Kazakhstan, facing
the Ural Mountains, remains nameless and free-roaming.

Some radio journalists are convinced I am the author of the quote
'Bliss was it that dawn to be alive' and then committed suicide.
They call me *Irony Jane*. I can't remember the last time
I combed my hair, let alone spoke, but the paparazzi call me
The Flash Gazelle. Farmers call me *Baby Burdock*
and, as a newborn, I was baptised by the silent movie ghost
of Leopoldine Konstantin who mouthed the words
Dear Elvina, thus I've met you once before
subsiding with the harpsichord into the floor.

Mothers

I thought I was the child in this scenario.
I played the child and you loved me.
I did a grumpy face when the university
took Mr Teddy Rag-Ears,
I got words muddled like, 'I stood very truck
as the still went through me.'

But then today
my future child called me on the telephone
and said, in a squeaky voice, 'My mum is dying,
can you come over, I need someone to talk to.'

I didn't know where my future child lived.
I had a feeling she was called Bertha
which disappointed me.

'I live in south east west London,' she said,
'Where the spies and the cleaners live.
It's spotless and seemingly empty.'

On the way over, a terrible pain ripped
through my stomach and I distantly
remembered a woman from my
adulthood I hadn't seen since
that bed-wetting dream.

I passed glass conservatories on Bertha's street.
They were acting as gallows for hanging plants.
'I like that image,' says Bertha, knotting the ties
on my hospital gown, shooing me out: 'I told you
no more running away from hospital, didn't I?'

Bertha, I went straight back. It's disappeared –
all except the scout-hut used for art therapy
that whiffs a bit. This is my picture of mummy:
that is a tree because she's in a forest, those are
mummy's pink gloves and that's an axe.

Snow Hotel

I

'It is time for us to get out of Switzerland'
you announced and I couldn't have agreed more

since we were not in Switzerland and my feet
were suffering in the clogs. My right hand

had been shot away in Bavaria and I refused
to employ my left hand for personal reasons.

We had moved to the fifth storey of the hotel.
Your chauffeur sang a message up the drain-pipe:

'There are many exciting opportunities arising
in the glove compartment,' which was code for

'Love has vanished from the world, better jump.'
I pulled the rip-cord of my winter parachute,

waved in the brusque air, like a strangely lovely
fevered shiver. People were still on the streets.

It was quite funny the way they'd carried on speaking,
standing outside burger joints, re-enacting a chat,

puffing on a 'fag', pretending to breathe – you have
never seen smoke so tremulous in its falling lace.

II

The following week you were passing moist-eyed
beside the once beleaguered lime chapel, moaning

about being typecast, 'I never even cry. My eyes just
get moist. Moist is the extent of my emotional range.

It's such a joke.' A guileless portico stuck to the face
of a filthy building dripped with rain: everything

was begging for love (women, harbours, plastic,
grapes, nuclear power plants, gym teachers) and

black tooth-marks were frosting the unused joints
of my left hand (which was not my helping hand,

although my right hand was declared a saint after it
was chopped off in Bulgaria) as your lips shaped out

'The sixth storey of the hotel would suit us perfectly.'
I had a suspicion we were crossing into Switzerland.

Unacceptable Language

Any similarity to persons living or dead is
purely coincidental, apart from Andy, you cunt,
there was never a house in St Tropez. Do you
realise Greta used a toasted sandwich machine
to straighten her hair? As for Sue, she can sod
off back to Norwich, all she ever did was whine
and moan about her abusive parents: so they hit
her with a bath loofah? Jemima was murdered
by those toffs, she swears she wasn't, but I've
seen her blue and bloated head buried in their
books. Gorgeously unclean, the twins are really
just one woman called Angela: some evenings
she thumbs me like a Holy Bible or Koran
or whatever, but mostly lies about stupid things
like can-openers or where the treasure is. Saul,
what were you thinking? She gained a degree
in avoidance addiction: seduce, revel and flee.
Jean needs a married man. She's not like you, Saul.
Where's your backbone, Florence? Being gay,
shouldn't you curb your racism? Perhaps rivers
don't flow like that, perhaps Dominic was right:
that baby belonged to nobody, it was a hoax,
a hoax in a pram to beguile him into empathy.
Empathy? That's a consumer tool if ever there
was a Mecca, which there isn't, otherwise what
are we doing in the supermarket? Meet me in
Greenwich village, Delilah, and we'll recreate
the sixties. Burn this bra. Is that right? No, burn
this chair. Is that right? What are we supposed to
burn again? I arrived for the revolution with my
lunchbox. There were sheep. You people promised
to be my loud generation. I regret everything.
Derek is a contented dentist.

Mystery Tears

A poem about hysteria

You could order them from China over the Internet.
The website showed a grainy picture of Vivien Leigh
in *Streetcar Named Desire*.
It was two vials for twenty euros
and they were packaged like AA batteries.

They first became popular on the young German art scene –
thin boys would tap a few drops into their eyes then
paint their girlfriends legs akimbo and faces cramped
with wisdom, in the style of the Weimar Republic. It was
sexy. They weren't like artificial Hollywood tears,
they had a sticky, salty texture
and a staggered release system. One minute,
you're sitting at the dinner table eating a perfectly nice steak
then you're crying until you're sick in a plant-pot.

My partner sadly became addicted to Mystery Tears.
A thousand pounds went in a week
and everything I did provoked despair.
She loved the trickling sensation.
'It's so romantic,' she said, 'and yet I feel nothing.'
She started labelling her stash with names like
For Another and *Things I Dare Not Tell*.
She alternated vials, sometimes
cried all night.

She had bottles sent by special delivery marked
Not Enough. A dealer sold her stuff cut with
Fairy Liquid, street-name: *River of Sorrow*.
Our flat shook and dampened. I never
touched it. Each day she woke up

calmer and calmer.

Method Acting

(sorry, Chekhov)

I was Nina from *The Seagull*
while everyone was just getting on with their lives.
'I am a seagull – no – no, I am an actress'
I'd say, then I'd weep. I was politely asked
to leave several Early Learning Centres.
There was no lake to wander by
so I drifted about by the fish counter in Tesco.
'Am I much changed?' I asked the woman.
She could not reply. 'Your hair-net
is the most melancholy thing I've ever seen,' I said.
I meant it as a compliment. I was asked to leave.
'God take pity on homeless wanderers,' I'd say
to a parked Land Rover, then I'd weep.

There was a young theatre director who loved me.
He stood like a beggar by the pick and mix section
of Cineworld. 'Why do you say that you have kissed
the ground I walk on?' I'd say, 'Would you kiss
the gridded stairs of an escalator? Would you kiss
a red stain on the floor of a crisis shelter?'

Once, in a summer pub – 'The Swan' perhaps
in Stratford or 'The Seagull', no, that's not right –
an older man squeezed lemon on my scampi.
Oh, older men! 'Your life is beautiful,' I said.
He drank his bitter ale like Agamemnon.
He told me a knock knock joke. My head reeled.
'To one out of a million,' I flirted, 'comes
a bright destiny full of interest and meaning.'
'You are very young and very kind,' he laughed.
I forgot all about my Cineworld boy.
My spirit grew. My face thinned.

Years later, in a peasant-class carriage
of Virgin Rail, I tried to recreate that joke.
It was something about an interrupting sheep,

an interrupting seagull – no – no, that's not what I meant.
My gestures were heavy and crude.
I cried Scwark instead of baaaaaaa. The pain!
The peasants pursued me with compliments but
I knew, by then, I was not golden. Some people
are built for greatness: they can tell a knock knock joke
with torrents through the heart. Have you forgotten,
Constantine, our childhood days of paper-rounds
and swiped milk-bottles? A kestrel for a knave...
A seagull – and yet – no.

'I love him. I love him to despair,'
I told the chemist. She gave me Strepsils.
Sometimes, I was beside myself with the possibility of fame.
I stood in Dixons and smiled, pointing at the shiny laptops.
I imagined I had been employed in a Dixons' advert.
I imagined I was on a television screen
with a million people watching.
My older man knew the managers of many department stores.
They did not want me for their adverts.
Not with my hollow eyes.

I started to dream, every night, of my Cineworld boy.
I dreamt he handed me a hotdog without recognition.
His eyelids were swollen like closed mussel shells.
Minutes after, I'd hear a popcorn machine explode
in a back room, grey butter everywhere. I am a seagull.
I am definitely a seagull. I saw Trigorin one last time
through the French windows. He was as handsome
and unapproachable as that first day. Still telling the same
knock knock joke, the same inspiration endlessly.
I might go bowling later, he said. His breeziness destroyed me.

I came back to the bridge, Constantine.
Do you remember that student play we did?
I was your muse and you were my chiselled visionary.
You refused to use the zoom button on the camcorder,
I believed we were making history. Now you work in Cineworld
and I am a seagull – no – no, I am an actress.
But the art we made, Constantine, it was so gritty, it was so real:

'I worked as an 'ooker daan the East End, me lovelies,
it's an 'ard life being an 'ooker 'cause punters sometaans
dan't pay up then who 'as to foot the bill to the ald pimp?
Muggins 'ere. How else cauld me gets ma 'eroin
to inject into me veins? Can't complain tho.
Where's me burger and chips?
Where's me copy of the Sun*?'*

I can do it now, Constantine, I can act.
Before, my accent was vulgar and stereotyped
but now my hands move fluidly and I flex her pain
through the muscles of my past. Is Trigorin here still?
Has he not gone bowling yet? I love him, Constantine,
I love him more than I used to. An idea for a short story.

There is a hole in the air. A small, perfect hole
in the air and the whole sky is cracked around it.
The gunshot noise came later, in memory. I was
already miles away, getting into character
for tomorrow. I was holding a packet of polo mints
between two fingers, puffing out cold breath, pretending
I was Lauren Bacall, smoking a Vogue.
Who gives a rat's ass about our creativity now? Curse
the lot of them. My boy is dead from love of me.
I am mad for love of someone else. Someone else
is forever enthralled by what's-her-face who plays
that Russian bird in *Coronation Street*.

Mea culpa, Constantine. Under the sapphire moon,
there will always be poets with throbbing notebooks
looking for Juliets with pharmaceutical party bags,
Ophelias in tie-dye tourniquets. Lucrative business –
tragic women. I could have been Portia or Beatrice.
I could have been the eldest of the Mundy sisters
in *Dancing at Lughnasa*, scattering chicken-feed
on the west coast of Donegal.

The Dry Well

In the dry light of morning, I return to the well.
You think you know the outcome of this story.

Sunshine is a naked, roaming thing like hurt.
A well is a chance embedded in the ground.

The well was dry yesterday and the day before.
You think you know the lot about sunshine –

an early bird knows sod all about perseverance.
Good people, you lay down your curling souls

on the dust and surrender. I swing my bucket.
If the well is dry today I will come back tomorrow.

A Dialogue between Artist and Muse

John Donne   A fly is a more noble creature than the sunne,
because a fly hath life and the sunne hath not

A fly   I find you extremely patronising

Hey Las Vegas

Hey Las Vegas, can nothing save us
from you? Hey bottle-bins and Tesco Metro,
Monday yawnings, flu symptoms, the station pub
at Waterloo. You're all Las Vegas
and I'm hooked on you.

Hey Las Vegas, you're a cheeky sausage
aren't you? Swapping my lovers while I'm under
the covers watching their tattoo change. Kisses begun
in the city of sin – be it York or Durham –
taste of you, Las Vegas.

Hey Las Vegas, can a Yorkshire lass match
her drinks with you? I built a bedroom casino,
bet my hotel Bible and lost a week. Just one, Las Vegas,
pinch of comatose, powder up the nose
and I'm a queen for you.

Hey Las Vegas, I wore my Elvis costume
for you, a curtsey in Wetherspoons from muscle
cramp: your promise, like a flung bouquet
off Humber Bridge, to break my fall
Las Vegas, like the A63.

Genesis

The people from the London suburbs don't believe in God.
We read books about slavery on American soil and relate
to the need for mental escape and concur that the homeless
get a raw deal and the kids in the state schools should get bikes,
free bikes or free books or something and we fall in love
pragmatically and suffer consequences like we pay our taxes
and everybody knows how a therapist makes his money.

The people from the British library don't believe in fate.
We drink coffee at the end of meals and sigh for the economy
and we cut ourselves in high school but now we have more dignity
and liberal education has airy-fairy elements and the newspapers
are wrong and vivid imaginations write 'Where am I?'
on Ouija boards.

The people from the West End theatres don't believe in heaven.
We eat bagels with smoked salmon and smoke electric cigarettes
and the afterlife is something cavemen invented to make sense
of death and we drive cars that are too big for us and everyone
gets divorced and we criticise each other's choices when we love
with all our hearts.

The people from the Oxford drinking establishments don't believe
    in ghosts.
We drink mulled wine at Christmas and Dickens
was sentimental and no one gets this far without a square set
of shoulders and pharmaceutical companies created our dysfunctions
and we could think our way out of a genocide situation and we
prove this every day in the darkness of our studies.

The people from the half-bought houses don't believe in karma.
We play tennis with tanned arms and come out to our parents and
wait for the backlash and never wear the same t-shirt twice
and apply for jobs we won't enjoy and have sex with our eyes open
and carry burning debts of duty and care about the war
occurring in our partners' heads.

The people from the city side of the river don't believe in elves.
We count to ten before we explode and observe the red axes
in the big glass cabinets that say 'break in case of emergency'
and we walk over wrought-iron bridges with little briefcases and
we never think about skipping and we keep our chins up
without the help of buttercups.

9 Possible Reasons for Throwing a Cat into a Wheelie Bin

The RSPCA has said it will be speaking to a woman caught on CCTV
dumping a cat into a wheelie bin in Coventry – BBC News

1) You mistook the cat for a crisp packet.
2) You believe the cat spoke to you and requested a lift to the inside of the wheelie bin.
3) You mistook the wheelie bin for a house.
4) You wanted the cat to relate to your own suffering.
5) The cat was on fire.
6) The wheelie bin was full of cream.
7) Your mother was a cat-lover and she hated you.
8) The owner of the cat put your child in a wheelie bin.
9) The cat was planning to steal your husband.

Day Room

Some crazy people believe they are Napoleon.
I am Alexander I of Russia, enthralled by Napoleon.
I declared, somewhat tardily, 'We can no longer reign together!'
after my small friend invaded me in 1812.

You think I'm joking.
Lip-chewing Meg is deluded about being Napoleon
but I *am* Alexander I of Russia, betrayed, muddled, conflicted.

This is not a metaphor. From my football coach
I learnt Rousseau's gospel of humanity, from my babysitter
I learnt the traditions of Russian autocracy and when I said

'The limits of liberty are the principles of order,'
what I really meant to say was:
I give up.

I'm taking my dying empress for a change of air.

Faith

The atheist is good in bed and debates.
Jacuzzis make the atheist uncomfortable, their public bubbles.
Numbers feel more theatrical around the atheist, listen:
TWO THOUSAND AND TWO.
ONE HUNDRED AND FIFTY FIVE. We sleep
as if our bodies are bound together with electric cables.

The Christian purifies me much like Klonopin
(or watching a large man ride a tricycle),
plays Spanish guitar with bleeding fingers
and we sleep as if we are hiding beneath a train.

I don't want to talk about the agnostic.
This game is dangerous and, anyway, I can't be bothered.

Like a wasp, the agnostic is surrounded
by dying comrades. Hospital beds and normal beds
all travel in the same direction, lugging our mothers
like rolls of Turkish carpet on their backs.
The agnostic lets me bitch about the atheist and the Christian.
We sleep as if we are alone.

'Do you think you're God?' the agnostic asked me once,
'You swallow pebbles to make your body lighter.
Someone lends you five pence and you fall in love.
You're like a medieval beggar without legs
pulled along in the dirt by your own needy smile.'

Maybe the agnostic didn't say that.
Let me sit for a minute quietly and gather my thoughts.

Dolores

Handfast on my other hand, it was
a sad and sinless way strung with
star-proof mirrors: I touched
no one and only a few touched me.

'Come on!' screamed the mistress and redoubled
her perfume. She was not prepared to rest
her forehead any longer on that kettledrum,
not unless you popped a tasty deathworm
in her tequila.

'I miss the way I used to call the shots around here,'
the first line of the ant-farm anthem.

'Arghhh,' I said, accidentally out loud
and the fair vast head of love
denied my feast-day.

There Once Was A Boy Named Bosh

There once was a boy named Bosh
who had a Shallow family. Daddy
Shallow dealt in motorcars, his favourite
word was 'repercussion' and he always
kept Mother Shallow in pocket if not
in peace. She was a narcissist who'd
perfected the wilting flower. Doctor
Shallow gave her pills for her nerves.
'We all have nerves,' said Bosh, but
Brother Shallow was found hanging
in the attic like an off light-bulb so
Grandma Shallow did the cooking
and Shallow neighbours constructed car-pools
to get Bosh to school. Teacher Shallow
collected money for nearly-dead children
in hot places and Bosh was supposed to
say a little something in assembly but
Brother Shallow was all-the-way dead
and where's his money? The Shallow girls
found Bosh mean and sexy when he got
blind with self-loathing. Mother Shallow
said, 'Why can't you play football?' because
she only cared about external achievements
and Daddy Shallow polished himself in his
dark Mercedes. 'It's like they are zombies,'
Bosh thought, 'Who don't have any blood:
eating their McDonald's onion rings, telling
me they're hurting too,' so Bosh started
drinking lots and lots of beer and whisky
like an adult does when he loses something
big like a poker game or a piece of paper
with a number on it. 'My Shallow family
are so Shallow,' Bosh said, 'they probably
wouldn't notice if I was hanged too,' and
Bosh was wrong about this, but Bosh put
a dressing gown cord round his neck as
Daddy Shallow watched *American Beauty*

downstairs and Sister Shallow swallowed
leeches in her bedroom to get skinny and
Mummy Shallow wrote in her pink leather diary.

Thoughts inside a Head inside a Kennel inside a Church

I had become increasingly
suspicious of those around me
especially after the kidnap attempt
and two masked soldiers raided my house.
I hid in the grandfather clock.

People noticed my language was no longer
one with the peacemaker of Europe.
I'd become addicted to my paramour's story,
I had specialist books out:

What My Paramour Thinks About So-called Liberal Reforms.
The Ninety-Nine Sleeping Positions of My Paramour (with Diagrams).
Instructions My Paramour Feels Your Dog Would Obey.

I couldn't smoke a cigarette
without apologising to the walls.

My friend set me up with sandwiches,
a flask of sugary tea
and helped me build the kennel:
'There is nothing more relaxed, more tranquil
than living alone in a kennel in a church.'

No more kidnapping scares
nor menacing phone calls. No unmarked jeeps
waiting in the street. I didn't receive
a Valentine's card saying 'no one likes you, love from us all'.

I couldn't stand up straight
due to the low roof. I'd run out of toffees
and what with no TV,
no Travel Scrabble, no rowing machine,
there was *literally* nothing to do
but pray.

The Only People in Paradise

Yours are the victories of light: your feet
Rest from good toil, where rest is brave and sweet:
But after warfare in a mourning gloom,
I rest in clouds of doom.

from 'Mystic and Cavalier' by Lionel Johnson

I'll have a laugh with Lionel Johnson in heaven
staying up to praise the plaintive asylum burning
in the first mellow bars of light. What a lovely way
to spend an afterlife, watching dark angels go by,
two players lounging by the ruinous church door.

I'll say hey Lionel, recognise these visions?
On earth, you made doom verse out of them.
Who knew, crunchy and delicious, they'd be
a tree of innocence with ashen apples on it?

And at the silent disco on Friday night, we'll whisper
'D.J. please... Drop. The. Beat', as the Fire Girls snake
the Twist o Flex of the Seraph, and Oliver Reed gets drunk.

Fantasy Role-Play

You had two children. They were present, like crickets,
too young to do anything but lie there and feel.
Your husband was a reactive blink to an inappropriate comment.
Your house was the shape of a lucky horse-shoe.
There were archways and guard dogs and roses. 'I love you,' I said
as you closed the door, screamed, opened it again, then silently
packed little Lionel and Greta into my car, stuffed your satchel
with apples from the tree you were married under
and got into the passenger seat.

We listened to 'Dig a Pony' by the Beatles
and sang, 'She can penetrate any place she goes!'
while the kids played rock-paper-scissors in the back.
You wouldn't let me kiss you for the first two weeks.
I had to wear a plastic Spider-Man mask.

One day, we were sitting in the Black Magic bar
of the Dawdle Bug hotel, wondering how to get
Lionel and Greta into private school. You looked so beautiful
drinking a pint of soda water with your big gloves on.
I said, 'Do you regret dropping your husband like that?
Leaving your perfect life? Sleeping on the road?'

'My name is Marcella,' you said,
'I worked as a maid in the Jeffersons' household.
The woman you loved was a cold and passive mother
and her husband was needy, disloyal and collapsible.
They were always fighting, throwing plates, cleaning products,
        fridges
at each other, mushing Lionel's face into his broccoli,
shunting Greta around like a mini vacuum cleaner.
When you arrived, I saw the chance to give them a better life.'

'Do you really think I can give you a better life?' I said.
'Look,' said Marcella the maid, 'Lionel and Greta
are so peaceful around us now. Lionel's like a tiny philosophy
        professor

34

and Greta's shadow puppets have a Rothko soul.
We're like the parents they were always meant to have.'

'I love you so much,' I said.
'I'm still very angry with you, Mr Jefferson,' you said.
'I know,' I said, breathing softly through my nose
as the sun came up on the Black Magic bar
and our battered faces. You bit into an apple.
'My name is not Mr Jefferson,' I said, 'I am their gardener, Alejandro.
Let's wake up the children and go home.'

Empty Nest

My home country has flourished
under the dictatorship of ABBA.
My son is studying the appreciation
of youthful male beauty at Poxthud,
the top university. My husband
chose to disappear and live the rest
of his life in anonymity. Painted
turtles use their vomeronasal organ
to smell underwater. There are
enforced breeding sessions.
The only thing my ventriloquist dummy
will say is 'I am not an effigy!' which
makes for pretty dire entertainment,
but the issue is not that. My therapist
and his friends made a short film called
The Lie is Dead. I'm either a brilliant
actress or a vacant chair.

Spat

'It's me or the dog,' she laughed,
though by 'dog' she meant 'void'
and by 'laughed' I mean 'sobbed'
and by 'me' she meant 'us'
and by 'she' I mean 'you'
and by 'or' she meant 'and'.
'It's us and the void,' you sobbed.

How the Wild Horse Stopped Me

I was punching in the last digit of your number
when a wild horse came up to me and said
'Would you agree gathering information is an important way
to help people make decisions?' 'I guess,' I said.

'So you'd agree surveys can help decide
where money should be spent, what products to purchase,
what problems there might be in the near and/or distant future?'
'Uh huh.' I tried again to dial.

'And your ideal survey... would it have A) Big questions B) Small
    questions. C) Stupid questions. D) Impossible questions?' 'I
    haven't time for this.'
The horse snorted in the manner of his species,
'I'll put you down for E) I just want silence in my head.'

'I. Am. Calling. My. Date. OKAY?'

The wild horse shook his dark mane. Stood aghast.
He gave a thespian whinny.

'Write your favourite colour on this scrap of paper then drop it in
    the fish bowl. Thanks. Now pick one from the bowl.'
'There's only mine in there.' 'Let's see! Let's see!'
'Purple.'
'We only accept primary colours. I'll tick blue and red...'

Do you ever go down to the river?
A) Not since mother/father/sister/brother/everyone went mental.
B) Not since I fell in love.
C) Not since I pretended to move on.
D) My face is wet with river water. I have a watermark across my
    chin.'

'B. No. C. No. C. No. C.'

'Which of the following questions could be described as "open ended":

1) Did you think I couldn't tell your eyes wrote patterns of
        yearning on my chest?
2) Is there a second hand on this watch?
3) Has nature ever been violent towards you when intoxicated?
4) Will you marry me – just once – before I die?'

The horse was not a normal horse.
He had a look, like a sexual predator.
Three months had passed and I hadn't called you.
You had found somebody else, or starved to death by the phone.

The wild horse was sobbing and soliloquising.
'Do you realise what I've sacrificed for your pointless survey?'
        I shouted.
'What survey? I'm a horse.'

The Island Woman of Coma Dawn

My feet dart in the water.
Like sad guitarist fingers.
I've come here to carve.

Such calm mineral caves.
Tomorrow Trojan ducks.
Will bob, quack in beeps.

I'm ridden from all love.
Distilled in exiled pause.
Weightless soul-case, free.

Sunrise in Coma Dawn is.
A timid rising in the air.
Eyelash chance of a kiss.

Then one breath of light.
Reborn up yesterday's pipes.
Stubs answers on my eye.

Jungle of parasols hears no.
Snores, no nosy footfalls, I can.
Defecate in orange groves.

2

The Truth about Camelot

If you love enough, you'll lie a lot.
Guess they did in Camelot.
– Tori Amos

Prologue

Mother Earth offers naked, shivering king
blanket of snow.
'Very funny,' he thinks, already
dead.

I

A Confident Local Youth

(Ten Years Earlier)

Hark! Goatherd approaches. Perhaps he bears

the coveted eggs of the Queen's wooden bird?
She is quite mad. Poor tart. I love her to bits.
She hires a midwife to watch her oven door –

'a secret love spawns a burning babe'. Witches
talk a lot of shit. Just another day in Camelot
where love is law and dragons swear in Welsh.

No sallow bus traveller hurls a custard cream
in fire-red mouths, spit! A clean cornet toots.
Jousting. Archery. Karaoke. I'd do anything

for love: talk where Meat Loaf minces round,
no loop-hole chorus. Ping-pong. Spit-roast
wild boar, fork holes punch, I want! I want!

II

Some Last Words

A faint Town Crier speaks to the sky:
'Yellow cannonball turban rainbow drop
in tunnel-sleeved dusk, sundial nods off,
good night town!' Unloads big hat, quiet
summer, lifts pistol to his brain, blows.

Rumour is they find another malformed boy
living on canned crayfish in his wishing well.
A fixer smoothes over Camelot suicides.
Villagers call him 'The Wolf'. He is a wolf.

Urchin Who Is Stalking Guinevere's Scullery Maid

God she's beautiful.
I think her face is the meaning of life.
The word 'scullery' is so dirty.
Have to stop chewing when there's nothing in my mouth.

Camelot Estate Agent

Unmarried live in mushrooms: R.T. squires,
cameo visions, magic-cloth tailors, two jolly
barmen (they alternate: law permits one paid
jollity per workplace. Disney season exempt
of-fucking-course). Well-lit one-bed shroom:
all mod cons, gilled floors for pacing suitors,
McLaren spore-print, a no-scary-face brass
door-knocker that confirms noteworthiness,
consolation fireplace, burnt old bramble bits,
love notes etc. Armchair with rocking options,
pearl-stitch snuggery, serene not lonely, spot-
less chimney, instant prayer-speed: whoosh!

(I sent up blank one there, as demonstration.)

V

Exiled Journalist Disguised as Shrub

Poky mushroom attic brings borderless
aura of homeliness? Maybe secret ambience

aerosols holding 'the Sunday Roast Virus'
are sprayed in ventilation system? No.

Such stunts would disrupt the habitat
of the Air-Vent Vermin: Scissor-limb freaks

herniated inside tunnels that, yesteryear,
were the band of lucky boys, gifted boys

hand-picked by The Great King Arthur
himself for 'His Holy Chivalric Order...'

Pre-Lancelot. Pre-circular desks.
Pre-riverboat tax on floating women,

there was one man with a crazy dream:
'King Arthur and his Crab-Boy Army'.

I say it only once. Don't believe me?
Ask any twitchy shrub.

VI

Arthur's Crab–Boy Vision Faces Scalpel Practicalities

In his laboratory, King Arthur is secretly attempting to combine a crab
with a boy to create 'Crab Boy', born wearing his own coat of arms.
Unfortunately Arthur is not a scientist and one can't simply chop off a
boy's hand and screw in a claw – as this blood-sprayed apron would attest.
His lucky boys are looking worse for wear. Hung upside down. I'd prefer
it if I didn't listen to this one…

*(Recording of Arthur in his crab-boy laboratory caught on
blind cleaner's Dictaphone while she whispered ideas for erotic
novels edited out for compassionate reasons)*

'All my maths checked out: 'Forwards of Man'
plus 'Sideways of Crab' equals 'Perfect Thinker'.
But bones won't merge ideas: mix beckoning claw

with half-cup opposable pink thumbs (human
body just spasm nerves blobbed in column) no
troops of amphibious damsels, no algae-beard

howls 'Mollusc! Mollusc!' in stoned pool, no
Crab born in Knight costume – just little boys without
hands. Maybe if I try. Give them bouncier knees.

The innocent never stop screaming. I'm trying to
make you into legends. Excuse me? Boy in blood,
did you just ask 'Why a Crab and Not a Lion?'

WHY A NOBLE CRAB? You little sacrilegious fu…'

Tape cuts out.

VII

Crab Quotes

*You can crab your way into the heart of God
if you're prepared to crab your way out again.*
Matthew

You know nothing about the sources of my honour.
A Crab

VIII

You

Somewhere along the line we started to believe
that mutilated boys were living inside the walls.

And now we are listening to a Raving King speech
beginning: 'Guinevere, everything is suddenly clear.'

IX

Raving King Speech

'Guinevere, everything is suddenly clear.

They dance crab-wise in synchronised formations,
very sarcastic rhythms. Pest control guns riddled
air-holes so their ghosts could breathe. Watch this:

as my pen moves they are writing the same word
backwards on the other side of the paper. Proof!
Loft scuffles in mutilated chirp. Inside the walls

they're mimics. We fall silent together. Stop crying
Guinevere. Celebrate discoveries. I mutilated boys
to make them look more like Crabs. I know I did!

We have been living in a fairy tale! I hate that huge
pointy hat you wear. That hat has made me impotent.
Have you cheated on me? You can say. I won't mind.'

Lancelot's Poetry Reading in Smoky Bar

(His stubble shows the slightest beginnings of Allen Ginsberg's beard)

Camelot, I have given you all and now I am everything.
Camelot, a room full of campaigning women is wetting stamps and
    throwing letters into the lake.
You know never to judge anything on the way it turns out.
There is no mailbox for the lady of the lake, is there Camelot?
You know things about the human heart the human heart can't
    even feel
like 'true love makes you lie which makes you honest to kindness
    which is love and love is truth'.
Camelot, Keats tried to paraphrase you.
Camelot, when will your factories cease the production of
    expendable brothers with rhyming names?
Camelot, I fell in love with a queen.
Merlin taped spoons to his hands and he prowls the forest diving at
    the eyes of eagles and always failing.
Camelot, I am adopted. There is mental illness in my family.
Camelot, I was a little boy raised in a magical kingdom by a woman
    made of water who could only touch by licking.
Camelot, I'm asking the difficult questions, not you.
Back the fuck off my blurry childhood Camelot it is not my spell.
Arthur must not die yet. I still want that interview.
Camelot, when will your mortal mermaids feel themselves clean?
Where is the holy grail?
They took it to paint it for a magazine and now it's disappeared.
Camelot, I don't want to be a monk who is alone forever just
    because she is a nun who is alone forever but this is the only
    symmetry left to me.
Camelot, symmetry is the last remnant of sexual desire.
I have made grave mistakes in the name of symbolism.
Camelot, the more miserable I get, the more handsome I become.
    If I ever commit suicide, a nation of women will orgasm
    simultaneously.
Camelot, lube up your cemeteries.

Camelot, the skies will crust with thick brown fluid
  and there will be acid rain storms.
Camelot, when I make love to her, I forget I am a man. Sorry.

XI

Arthur, Arthur, Arthur...

Scene. A mad and bedraggled Arthur sits alone in a dim cobwebbed garret, staring hard at the wall, consumed with guilt for everything he has ever done or thought during his entire life.

King Arthur tells dead boy in wall: you're not alone.
Dead boy in wall tells Arthur: that's nice of you to say.

King burns his eyes straight across any level on wall.
Boy feels faint warmth run course from other side.

On another level of wall King burns a straight eye-line.
From other side Boy runs same course for warmth.

Straight line burns across King wall any level on eye.
Burns a thin road Boy can run across until cold.

They follow each other's eyes very closely in darkness.

XII

A Disgruntled Knight

*(Not mentioned in a book or a poem or anything ever,
even in this poem I had to make up all the details)*

My armour is not polished: I am not a poster boy.
I make the ugly red-brown stains on the battlefield.
The celebrity knights only stay for the fanfare
then make a big show of leaving purposefully –
'What's that you say? Knights with blow-dried hair
needed urgently for an Easter Egg hunt? Come on boys!'
Some have ten-year contracts as romantic leads,
can't lose a fingernail let alone a leg. Later they'll
canter back to the castle cheering, waving a flag
and our people will sleep tight as Camelot falls.

This is pretend war. I feel pretend hate. Unicorn!
Unicorn! My kingdom for a unicorn!
Someone still has to stay here and die.

3

Sea Bed

I continue slow and clear in my broken images.
– Robert Graves

Damage

Her teddy bear eloped with her mother.
Her father went to buy flowers for himself
on Father's Day and never came home. Her grandma
was a waste-paper basket. She was raised by staplers.
Her skin was deathly white. Her birthmark
was the shape of Africa. No one explained
anything to her. She excelled at school until
she was abused by her own calculator. She ran
away from home to join a troupe of travelling
accountants. She could balance a Filofax on her head
and yawn at the same time. Audiences loved her.
She married a man called Jerry, who turned out to be
a hat-stand in disguise. She contracted a disease
transmitted by celibacy. She slept in a violin case, smoking
rosin. She lost all pleasurable sensation in her ears.
She drank to forget. She drank to remember where
she'd left her bike. I met her during the winter.
She said, 'I need someone to save me.' I did
what any sensible person would have done. I did
what any sensible person would have done.

This Was All About Me

No one ever betrayed me.
This was all about me.
You were missing nothing.
I refrained from disclosure.
You heard very little indeed.

It was important to me.
They were weak to insist.
You heard very little indeed.
We had a fair shot, kinda.
There was the little matter of.

You heard very little indeed.
This couldn't transform in full.
You had your foot on it.
This was certainly the first.
I predicted but too soon.

They were on to us before.
Don't presume you're integral.
The middle wasn't eaten then.
This happened while they slept.
You heard very little indeed.

They didn't care for someone.
You heard very little indeed.
We held hands in fiction.
I intended to tell you straight.
You had many, many names.

This was without internal reference.
I was fully dressed throughout.
You heard very little indeed.
The foreigners understood it.
We never charged for air.

I breathed out all your smoke.
This occurred in the summer of.
You heard very little indeed.
These moments meant everything.
I couldn't have reached out.

The station was far from the ocean.
You heard very little indeed.
They were not vital to proceedings.
The outcome was written.
I was wearing black at the time.

2:19 to Whitstable

I'm leaving once I've pick-axed this widowed moss.
I'm leaving once I've asphyxiated these doves.
I'm leaving once I've shaved my legs to smithereens.
I'm leaving once I've tidied this cupboard.
I'm leaving once I've practised my aloof walk.
I'm leaving once the Anti-Christ has finished his tea.
I'm leaving once I'm satisfied your sister's okay.
I'm leaving once the spare-ribs have digested.
I'm leaving once wallpaper comes in the shade of morose.
I'm leaving once my dignity has truly gone and not just nipped out
     for crisps.
I'm leaving once they've brought back hanging.
I'm leaving once the Palestinian thing is cool.
I'm leaving once inanimate objects get the vote.
I'm leaving once Norwegians achieve equal daylight.
I'm leaving once my grandma attends gay pride.
I'm leaving once there's no more creaking doors.
I'm leaving once your ex-lovers all die.
I'm leaving once the car is fully submerged.
I'm leaving once I've flirted with crack cocaine.
I'm leaving once it's never been this good before.
I'm leaving once I'm certain there's not a single kiss left in you, not
     even a stolen one whilst momentarily distracted by a wasp.
I'm leaving once I've sicked out a life-long supply of poems.
I'm leaving once my children have gone senile.
I'm leaving once the hospitals have been closed down by health and
     safety.
I'm leaving once I've cow-tipped this cathedral.
I'm leaving once my liver's poked by scientists.
I'm leaving once all the whites and the blacks and the young and
     the old and the deaf and the mute and the blind and the rich
     and the poor *literally* stand under the same umbrella.
I'm leaving once I've observed a drastic change in body
     temperature.
I'm leaving once the photographers have given up.
I'm leaving once heaven is empty because I've put everyone off it
     with my constant yelling up the rope-ladder.

I'm leaving once I've proved my subtle valiance.

I'm leaving once you've stopped doing whatever it is that you're
    doing, yep yep.

I'm leaving once the vegan jungle.

I'm leaving once the heavenly bond of (one orgasm that's all I'm
    asking dammit).

I'm leaving once I can't speak for the pain.

I'm leaving once your friends start calling me diddums.

I'm leaving once (you didn't realise I was this serious did you?).

I'm leaving once we've shared a tropical Calippo without the
    cinematic sense of the last bearable day on earth.

I'm leaving once (if you're waiting for the by-the-bye I don't think
    I can muster the strength).

I'm leaving once we've entered the 676th stage.

I'm leaving once Wake Up LA in Dulwich.

I'm leaving once our agents have fallen in lust.

I'm leaving once I've been cast as the painted whore in an
    Almodóvar film.

I'm leaving once we swoon through the commercials as well as the
    killer lines.

I'm leaving once there's an Oscar buzz around your psychologist.

I'm leaving once I've bitten into the syrup of a quiet drama.

I'm leaving once the looking glass only lets teetotallers through.

I'm leaving once the rhinestones reach their highest monetary
    value.

I'm leaving once I've caught my crying mother in my arms.

I'm leaving once a small incision under the lobe.

I'm leaving once my crown comes back from the cobblers.

I'm leaving once this affair makes one of us a necrophiliac.

I'm leaving once you've vomited down the phone and I've got it
    right in the ear.

I'm leaving once you've licked off my varnish and disliked my
    natural wood.

I'm leaving once you're the only person I've ever told this to.

I'm leaving once your soil-clods smash my window.

I'm leaving once you've hung me upside down for seven years then
    drained my head with a turquoise syringe.

I'm leaving once we all get a thing for turquoise syringes.

I'm leaving once you've been bludgeoned to death like Joe Orton.

I'm leaving once I no longer taste of cigarettes, chewing gum, hope.

Break-up Party

Everybody had a throat and none were gulping.
Presently came another man with drinks.
In the manner of tedious mingling, it was easeful enough.

It was only a tad draughty and always
abundant with firewood. That is to say, no one
ever mentioned the roof had been blown off.

There was little of the sobbing and song-writing about birds
one usually finds in these places, rather how
frank it was, how open.

'I was going to offer you representation,'
said a camp lawyer, stripping to his boxers for a dip
in the pool, 'but I see that won't be necessary.'

Sometimes I wished you would show me
something, just a nod or a wave of a glove.

Two Cents

Shingle the pages of *King Lear* with tears
of delighted laughter. Never cease
to amaze them with your sloth.

Take commitment-phobes out for tapas,
give no option but the croquettes.

Don't reply to letters
except to say: *'I've been mutilated
by a flung hedgehog. This is not a joke.'*

Encase the telephone in jelly and fist it.

Love the soiled bit. Look three ways
before gouging. All's fair in drove at wall.

Run

If my language was water
it would be rainwater

no-flow in bucket, gutter,
brow, no-flow in dust,

liquid thunder crumbed
in clay, sludge afraid

to slip away, since clouds
spewed out heroes,

water-babies, sent like slop,
like lava, fevered blood.

At night, downstream culverts
bundle their passage

back underneath a train,
a road, a city wall:

can't you hear the sound
of that old drowning song?

If the bedrock sings along:
job's a good 'un

but drainage systems spin
in dreams and bits resurface like

'percolate', 'swale', 'dinghy',
'sloop'; surf boards glitter

with buzz words, beaches
blotted in lisps of 'luff'

under a speaking moon:
'I dream to keep you yet

cursed to neap you! Alas,
but my hands are tides.'

She laps me, gulp, laps me
not. If my pleading was water

I'd be heading for you, top
news bulletin, forecast

world over: babe grab a
coat, zip up, storm's coming.

Sea Bed

He cared. But he didn't care enough
to stop taking the drugs when she said,
'I'll wait outside in the rain until you've finished.'

She cared. But she didn't care enough
to stop pulling his leg when he said,
'My leg is connected to my penis.'

He cared. But he didn't care enough
to defend her honour in the pub when Dave
said she did it Greek-style in an alley once.

You cared. But you didn't care enough
to keep walking when my pleading was just
reflex mouthings of a guillotined head.

He cared. But he didn't care enough
not to smash her apartment with a cricket bat
when she slept with a boyish girl.

We cared. But we didn't care enough
to wear eye-patches over our magnets when
we set our compass for one final paddle.

Public Detectives

I've been listening to your day through the wall
of a whole city. Sometimes the wires cross and I listen
to an old Taiwanese woman muttering to her cats.
I've been eavesdropping on your progress
with a glass tumbler pressed to a Tube map.
I've been conferring, finally, with the other reluctant troubadours:
they've sent single red roses to half the population
and still no girlish stammer from those macho dialling tones.
It's as if no one's listening except us.

You've been watching through the keyhole
of a scientific discovery. Sometimes the light flips and
you watch a dying puppy staring longingly at a sausage.
You've been measuring our time apart in guilty shrugs
when silent crowds mention me. You've been conferring,
finally, with the other burdened troubadours:
they've sent boxes of ice to half the population
and still no macho dialling tones from those girlish stammers.
It's as if no one's listening.

Facts

(from Philip Levine)

The Butterscotch Pot de Crème offered at Gjelina restaurant
in Venice, CA, is insanely delicious. In her Death Row fantasy
Nadia chose Butterscotch Pot de Crème for her last meal: 'And
I'd have Arabian food and fish and chips to remind me of home.'

The best way to smuggle pills from Mexico is within the bodies
of dead lobsters. Hide the dead lobsters in a bucket of fresh,
snapping ones (lobsters stay alive for 24 hours out of water) and
the police won't rummage around. Their dogs will smell fish.

I am not American. At twelve, I smoked roll-ups on the aerial
footbridge of How Stean Gorge in my dad's brown leather jacket
with my hair dyed the colour of suitcase. The pub in Masham
serves Sunday lunch and their specialities include lobster bisque.

In 2010, Tiger Woods checked into the Meadows in Wickenburg,
Arizona, to be treated for sex addiction. 'It's drugs, not sex,' says
the *National Enquirer*. Woods made no mention of his drug habit
in his 13-minute apology speech. The *Enquirer* may be lying to us.

There were no ticket barriers at Deptford station in the fall of 2009.
The grocer's opposite the Albany Arts Centre sells the retro sticks
of Wrigley's spearmint gum. No sugar-free pellets. 'Get a little closer'
is a slogan shared with Arrid Extra Dry deodorant. I flew to Atlanta

on the anniversary of John Lennon's death. My ex-fiancée works
at the Southbank Centre with my mother, and my friend Sarah has
played guitar in the Queen Elizabeth Hall and the Albany, I think,
but none of them knew about dead lobsters hidden amongst live ones.

The *Enquirer* would profit from a Tiger Woods drug orgy. Mr4Guv
from the ABC blog writes, 'My two neutered male dogs are
        mounting
one another all day long. Does that make my dogs sex addicts?' Yes.
I was muzzled for whispering 'I do not crave your blood' into a bag.

I told two lies in the last stanza. I crave blood. I do. A poet told me
love was an oral fixation. Watch my lips: it's not an oral fixation.
That's something else. That's a glory hole sucking on a long sentence.
I wooed with words. They loved an idea. Their idea was disproved.

The calmest I've ever been was in a sensitive room in Venice, CA.
I had a blue wallet with white lettering that said, 'Delay No More',
Nadia drank redemptive coffee with her ex-boyfriend while I was
assembling a designer cardboard house for a kitten to sleep in.

On the edge of North America, the citizens train their street-lights
to be respectful of madness. Like a row of woken trees, they shine
on the woman who guards the automatic doors singing 'they have
freed you!' and they shine on me, pushing the button to cross over.

I will never return to the butterscotch sands of Santa Monica or
the communal ash-trays of Walnut House where the misfits whooped
my name. I haven't the cash or the energy. Not even for Nadia,
whom I adore. Not even for one last meal of clean, American
        lobster.

To Whom It May Concern

If you see a lemon being cut, it is goodbye.
If you see an old and childish book, this is goodbye.
If you see a turtle on the television, a shot of rum
or two small winters, we are goodbye.
If you see a pain in the heart of the chalk,
goodbye is this, this white mark.

Screening

After watching a film about masked goblins
I sat you at the bar and told the truth.

I said, Sweetheart.
I said, Love of this season.
I said, Anything you can think of that's perfect.
Then I said, Malcontent. I said, Lothario.
Then I said, Barefoot in the seedling glass.

You said, Darling.
You said, Decades of child.
You said, Everything you can think of that's gentle.
Then you said, Rejection slip. Then, Worldwide prism.
Then you said, My other jacket is thin air.

The Promises

I gave up my seat at the bar
and I went to buy a goat.

I sold my goat to a farmer
who gave me three gold coins.

I placed those three gold coins
in the hands of a simple beggar.

The beggar flurried his rags,
revealed himself a prince.

The prince repaid my kindness
with a chest of diamonded robes.

My queenly garments caught
the eye of a roving captain.

We sailed to an empire where
they only spoke two words.

'You are…' said the natives and
their leader said 'You are…'

'You are… You are…' they sang
like bottle-flutes, 'You are…'

My captain heard a compliment
but I was not so sure.

That night we slept in velvet
or seaweed bathed in oil.

I dreamt I taught the trees
to bear rare, human fruit

with perfect hands and perfect
toes and not one hole.

In the morning, flower women
washed our feet in tin bowls.

The captain looked so happy
he wanted to be married

'neath an awning wrought of silver
like the colour of his sword.

'You are...' he said, 'You are...
rest your foot upon my heart.'

'I am *what*?' I challenged him,
'A liar, a waste of space?

Are you calling me a whore?
Are you calling me a rat?'

'You are...!' he moaned in panic,
squeezing love juice from his eyes

as the girls waved sprigs of magic
that honeyed on the tongue,

the native men crooned quick-time
but the lie had met the light:

the goat, the coins, the beggar prince,
this captain and these fertile dreams...

Where was my favourite wooden stool?
My smallness and my plan?

So I declined my promised land,
I flipped my God one last '*You* are...'

I took my seat at the bar.

Say When

I'm not a fan of red wine
but I'd drink anything with you.
A pint of bleach. Perhaps

I'd spit the red wine out
into a plant-pot? I can't drink
anything with you. Nothing.

A truthful drunk face will tempt
a guilty tender kiss. I build this
on nothing with you: everything

depends on wine. I won't kiss
anything on your truthful face,
a pint of lies, just do nothing.

You like red wine or white wine,
anything. I am something to you.
I am not nothing, but

Kissing

Like two teardrops racing down opposite faces
of the same hypocrite, their separate fabrications
form a single pool of clothes.

They are kissing to share the blame.
They are kissing to confuse their dental records.

If not tomorrow,
one of them must wake to be the one
unpicking from the plan, sliding out
from the tower of anniversary cards

onto the flat road. They are kissing to delay
the string of paper dolls asking to be real boys
and real girls. They are sucking the sting
from the lips that someday
will blurt

and, like surfacing from a cinema in mid-afternoon,
will meet the daylight scandalised.

What Shall We Do With Your Subconscious?

I'm tired of watching the riots and knowing
which young boys will be bodies by sundown.
I saw the bomb growing in the womb. I saw
you run and run and run while you kissed me.

I'm tired of playing cards with money that's
already gone and the drugs kicking in during
an exam I'm bound to pass and not just pass
but take charge of. I was and am a golden girl

in the past tense of the present tense, the drink
will lose your mind and there's no such thing
as a pre-emptive strike: can't you see the ash
falling on your yellow omelettes? It's a kind

of gift, they say, but callings are supposed to
call you somewhere. I'm tired of schoolyards
chequered with pre-pubescent bankers who'll
attempt to hang themselves once. This plane

has many dangling oxygen masks like a tree,
like a crashing tree. Do you understand me?
I saw prostitutes in wheelchairs by the pool
but this city won't burn, it will refuse to burn

for the sake of occasional happiness. Blimps.
Pistachios. Holding hands. I cannot foresee
you holding my hand yet I hear the evening
cockerel and I'm tired of the singing graves.

Limerence

n. Psychol. the state of being infatuated or obsessed with another person, typically involuntary, and characterised by a strong desire for reciprocation of one's feelings but not primarily for a sexual relationship.

Our criminal career was little more than
a series of movements.

Medicine

My head says soon
My heart says, when?

My head says one
My heart says ten

My head says skin
My heart says soul

My head says stuffed
My heart says whole

My head says willing
My heart says slave

My head says risky
My heart says brave

My head says breathe
My heart says snort

My head says saved
My heart says caught

My head says mend
My heart says lie

My head says policy
My heart says spy

My head says addict
My heart says, who?

My head says cynical
My heart says true

My head says fed
My heart says fat

My head says insecure
My heart says prat

My head says episode
My heart says life

My head says lover
My heart says wife

My head says children
My heart says, how?

My head says ambulance
My heart says now

My head says telephone
My heart says please

My head says hands
My heart says knees

My head says miracle
My heart says, when?

My head says snort
My heart says ten

My head says telephone
My heart says spy

My head says caught
My heart says lie

My head says stuffed
My heart says fat

My head says risky
My heart says prat

My head says ambulance
My heart says please

My head says policy
My heart says knees

My head says breathe
My heart says brave

My head says cynical
My heart says slave

My head says addict
My heart says soul

My head says soon
My heart says whole

My head says lover
My heart says true

My head says insecure
My heart says, who?

My head says children
My heart says wife

My head says miracle
My heart says life

My head says mend
My heart says, how?

My head says willing
My heart says now

Izzy

Everybody in the village was weaving baskets
for the annual basket fair.

Izzy was sitting on a bale of hay looking at her basket.

There was an old woman weaving next to her
with a shawl over her hair and oversized
wooden clogs on.

This old woman was absorbed in her basket-weaving.

Izzy looked at the basket she'd just finished,
then at the woman, then at the sun,
then around the square at the villagers – young and old,
in their clogs, lost in their basket-weaving – then
back at her own basket.

She picked it up and set it on her knee.

Conqueror

Do you remember, darling, the time
when no one said 'No'? But they did,
you know, in private as you stole
the show in another town, they said
'No' to themselves, they abandoned you
repeatedly in the long halls, they said
'No' to their well-being, they found a way
to hide their 'No's' behind great smiles
because they loved you, but love,
you know, is not the same as 'Yes'. Yes,
they let you win because your need
to win was vast. They felt your flag
in their heads and the blood making
pictures but their eyes weren't shut,
you know, and their eyes, their loving
eyes were saying 'No'.

Atheism

I got down on my knees this afternoon –
I'd banged my right knee on the bed frame
the night before so my bruise twanged
slightly against the floorboards.

I entwined my fingers
like people do in church and I closed
my eyes. I said, 'Hey' and I said, 'Please',
and I suggested a deal.

I said, 'I'm not trying to mess with you,
I'm just asking
because this is all I want.
Give me this and I will
believe in you. I will chuck my bottles
in the bin. I will help the needy.
I will live a healthy life in the grip of truth.
Just let it happen tonight. Let me do
nothing and let it happen to me, because
I'm beyond the point where I can
make a single move. Thanks a lot. Please.'

Then I said, 'Please' a few more times,
then I stood up and went
to brush my teeth before I left the house.

I'm Sorry This Poem Is So Painful

I was treated for fairy-godmother dependency.
I arrived with a crate of leaving presents:

a cling-film sculpture of fog from Mother Urge,

a permanent-marker of smoke from Mother Longing,

a murmur in a Tupperware box from Mother Promise,

and five skinned prawns from Mother Hope
(in case I got peckish for a bite of almost nothing).

The first thing my healers did
was confiscate my hamper.

★★★

They sat me with a group of human protégées.
Their skulls like mine bore fluorescent scars
from the tap-tap-tap of magic wands.

Mother Numb made the best aspartame cheesecake.
Carcinogenic, it tasted like heaven.

'Is there Sweet'n Low for my coffee?' I asked,
'I just need a pinch of Sweet'n Low.'

'We came into these rooms,
broken by desire…' said the speaker,
pale behind a black lectern.

His facial skin was slack
with protruding beige teeth-marks, like his brain
had grown a mouth and started chewing its way out.

'Can I please have some fucking sweetener for my shit coffee?'
I asked again.

They spoke of hands briefly leafing through their hair,
a kiss on the cheek that might have been the wind,
'These are our honeyed moments,' they said,
'and they are not enough to live on.
They are not enough to keep us sane.'

The Stock Exchange

You can have my body, that's the least of my worries.
I gave my body to the awful and the sanitary
in the hope I might get something for my mind.
Just a peanut.

She offers her mind, that's the least pressing concern.
She gives her mind to the intellectual rugby club
in the hope she might get something for her body.
Just a thumbprint.

He chucks out his safekeeping, that's the least of his talents.
He gives his safekeeping to a city of hollow trees
in the hope he might get something for his gut.
Just a bead of sweat.

I gave my love, that's the least empty of my reserves.
I gave my love to the pretty and unhealthily pink
in the hope I might get something for my heart.
Just a companionable moment to myself.

The Last House

At the last house on the block, we smoke religiously.
We Google who we were in previous lives.
I was born in 'the territory of modern North Canada'.
You were a shoemaker in AD 375.

At the last house on the block, we talk of romance.
The loves outside these walls had misty breath.
We are demistified and now our breath is lonely.
No one ever saw the pain we couldn't feel.

At the last house on the block, we snack on pretzels.
Our nonsense is the source of much debate.
We sit in groups and rave about the boredom.
I'd a sweetheart once who swore by the human will.

I have a kindness hidden in my gym sock.
It's all I have to barter with your feats.
The intellectuals and whizz-kids back in London
think I'm frozen in amber like a fly.

But I have snared a person in my future,
a person who knows the secret knock
and the password which is just a cough or splutter
outside the doorway of the last house on the block.

At the last house on the block, we all have kindness
unused, in perfect nick, hung round our necks.
This kindness is our key back to the garden.
When our noses finish bleeding, we'll head back

with a message from the molehills: 'she was wrong
and he was wrong and I was wrong', and death
will be poured in moderation and my good side
and your good side will join with slight abandon.

The Fun Palace

(Commissioned for the Olympic Park, London)

One

It is a love story. Joan and her theatre workshop.
They found a crumbling slum in E15. They slept
illegally in the eaves like ghosts. She created
Oh, What a Lovely War. She shovelled rubble
from Angel Lane. She said, 'Let the waters close over me.'
She was an outsider. She grafted. She changed the world.

Two

It is a love story. Joan and her theatre workshop.
They rehearsed in a graveyard while bombs were falling.
She loved a ripper. A ripper is a miner who breaks new tunnels
out of stone. He almost got a lion cub into Ormesby Hall.
Gerry stood in front of bulldozers to save the Theatre Royal.
She tore up scripts. She guffawed. She changed the world.

Three

It is a love story. Joan and her theatre workshop.
She directed *Macbeth* at school. She plunged
the fake sword into the hidden butcher's meat,
the Mother Superior fainted. Joan wanted a university
of the streets. No cup and saucer hats. She chain-smoked.
She said, 'To hell with them.' She changed the world.

Four

It is a love story. Joan Littlewood and her theatre.
She was blacklisted from Broadcasting House.
She knew that two tons of coal equalled more
than two ounces of cheese. The Fun Palace was never built
on the banks of the River Lea. She almost cracked it.
She kicked the bucket. She changed the world.

Marriage of Equals

You hated the theatre and I hated the museums.
I didn't notice the butterflies.
You didn't notice the homeless.
I felt oppressed by Auden's old boy study castles.
You planted sapling projects in grey rockeries.
I got obsessed with poignant lines of graffiti.
You understood Oyster cards and booking in advance.
I had to wrench my head back from cauldrons of wine.
You had one beer in contentment.
My friends were idealists who started off yodelling.
Your friends were realists who started off hissing.

Your world was steadily increasing.
My government didn't exist.
You felt the bank balance of the nation in the tips of your fingers.
I bought rare, coffee-spoilt poetry books with crippled spines
from extortionate magpies in Iowa.
You saw the good in Thatcher.
I watched Ken Loach films in a dark room warmed
by the ghost of my grandfather's Yorkshire coal.

I could take or leave the planetarium.
You collided with Andromeda in your insomnia.
I was fine with pills.
You defied shrinks with your in-house mental janitor.
I sat down on the Tube when travelling just one stop.
You would never buy mystery meat from a backstreet 'all you can eat'
buffet called 'Puff the Chinese Dragon'.
I had never bought a sprig of ginger.
You blamed Gordon Brown for the future death of the sun.
I blamed the Rich in general while snacking
on a bite-size cube of decorated fruit cake.

I thought of Kirsty MacColl at Christmas.
You thought of your father's erratic moods.
I jogged alone on the treadmill in front of a mirror.

You punched the air with your lacrosse stick in school year-group
    photos.
I let potential serial killers use my bathroom after closing time.
You always packed a toothbrush.
I owned every Mike Leigh, even the early BBC television stuff.
You found *Career Girls* over-acted and plotless.
I wept outwardly for a week, inwardly for a year.
You didn't know who Adrian Mitchell was.
I couldn't assemble a pop-up tent.

You wouldn't let anyone read your self-penned screenplays.
I recited poems I wrote yesterday in busy restaurants
to embarrassed olive-skinned companions.
You read Sherlock Holmes novels in small print with a magnifying
    glass.

Your mum said, 'Go get your girl.'
My mum said, 'Stop proposing to slender-necked lampposts.'
You plunged the knife deeply and once.
I supported huge government funding for chocolate sculptures.
You audibly scoffed during my one-act *Hoodie Hamlet*.
I had a subtle nervous twitch triggered by memories of candlelight
and Leonard Cohen's 'The Partisan'.
You built Jerusalem on England's green and pleasant land.
I reinvented the fish pun.
You closed up like the magic portal.
I took the long slide down into the pool.

Corine

Corine is married now. Let her pass.
She's found a fireside decoration
that talks back. And a gold thread
of spit from her mouth to another's.
Someone to pass the salt. Someone
who'll make her a mother. Corine is
settled now. Let her be. She's found
a dolphin to swim with, a post on
which to lean. Lord knows she's waited
patiently. You knew this day would
come. Why so despondent? Hold on
to the edges of your eyes; don't cry.
Corine is happy. Now say goodbye.